10 Steps to Landing Your Dream Job

# 10 Steps to Landing Your Dream Job

**C. Renee McLain**

**10 Steps to Landing Your Dream Job**

© 2017 by C. Renee McLain

ISBN:  978-1546647164

Published by:  McLain Publishing

Printed in the United States of America

# DEDICATION

This book is dedicated to all successful job seekers everywhere. Whether you are just starting out in your career, seeking to go to the next level in your career, or transitioning to a new career, this book is for you. It will help to catapult you further in your endeavors as you progress towards your desired outcome. As you utilize this book as your personal workbook on your journey to Landing Your Dream Job and beyond, THINK BIG, PREPARE and ENGAGE.

# ACKNOWLEDGEMENT

First and foremost, I thank God for giving me the mindset to Encourage, Enlighten and Empower job seekers in their efforts of pursuing and obtaining their desired Dream Job. I thank my husband Robert J. McLain, Sr. who supports me in all of my endeavors. I am also grateful for the experience I have obtained throughout the years of my career to be able to apply it and impact the lives of others.

# 10 Steps to Landing Your Dream Job

10 Steps to Landing Your Dream Job

# CONTENTS

10 Steps to Landing Your Dream Job

## Step 1 - Have a Positive Mindset

Before you even begin the process of Landing Your Dream Job, the first and foremost step is to have a Positive Mindset. Your Mindset is so very important. You must embark on this journey knowing beyond the shadow of a doubt, that your end result of Landing Your Dream Job will happen. Think positive thoughts about it. Say positive statements to yourself. Declare and decree that you will obtain your Dream Job! Know that this accomplishment is achieveable and within your reach!

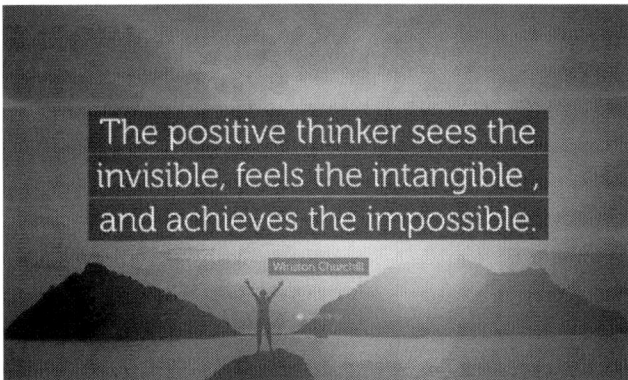

## Step 1 - Action Plan

**Do I have stinking thinking?  If so, what must I do to overcome this?**

**Am I ready to explore my desired career and stop working unfulfilling job after job?**

**What *is* my desired career?**

**What am I good at?**

**What do I love/like to do?**

**What do I feel I was born to do?**

**Do I really believe I can Land MY Dream Job?**

> **Confidence** *is your best accessory.*

*Never leave home without it.*

# Step 2 - Establish a Professional Email Address and Online Presence

This statement may seem unnecessary to some, and trivial to others, but it is very important to use a professional email address when applying for your Dream Job. Sexymama@gmail.com, and BigDaddy@gmail.com are not professional emails that you want to display on your resume and have a prospective employer use to contact you. Chances are they will not. An appropriate email address can simply be a combination of your name, so that it corresponds with your name, thereby making it easy for your prospective employer of your Dream Job to be able to identify you. For example, John F. Smith, can be:

john.f.smith@gmail.com
johnfsmith@gmail.com
jfsmith@gmail.com
smithjf@gmail.com
smithjohnf@gmail.com

Ok, you get the picture. In order to Land Your Dream Job, you must present yourself in a professional manner before you even apply for the position.

You must keep in mind your Online Presence when searching for your Dream Job. Does your Facebook, Instagram, Twitter, etc. profiles portray you as a positive professional? Do you display lewd pictures? Do you engage in controversial topics regarding religion or politics? Employers are interested in how one presents himself or herself, not only in a professional manner, but also in social and casual circles as well. So be mindful of what you post, where you post and how you post, before you post.

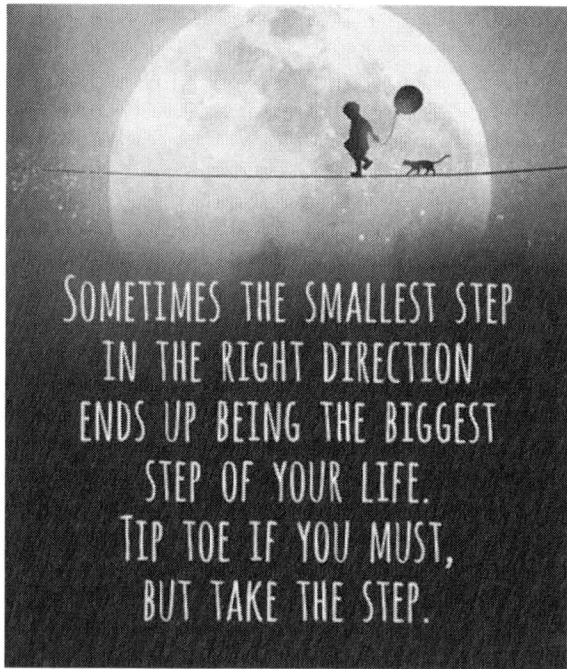

SOMETIMES THE SMALLEST STEP
IN THE RIGHT DIRECTION
ENDS UP BEING THE BIGGEST
STEP OF YOUR LIFE.
TIP TOE IF YOU MUST,
BUT TAKE THE STEP.

# Step 2 - Action Plan

**Do I need to update or change my professional email address?**

**Do I need to clean up my social media pages?**

# 10 Steps to Landing Your Dream Job

# Step 3 - Update Your Resume

Your resume is a tool. Think of it as a marketing document and not an autobiography. It must be strategic and professional. Your name and contact information, including your email and the one best phone number should be displayed at the top. You may also include your LinkedIn profile URL. There is no longer a need to share your street address because prospective employers will contact you via phone or email. This will also help cut down on identity theft. You may choose to share the city and state in which you reside, which is sufficient.

There are two main types of resumes, a functional resume and a chronological resume. Employers prefer the chronological resume, as it lists employment history information in a descending (most recent to least recent), easy to read format.

A career summary or objective is outdated and has been replaced by a well-branded headline. This headline should tell readers who you are professionally in regard to your current career objective. You may also want to add one or two subheadings to further define your expertise. Your employment history should be in descending order, meaning current or most recent position listed first. Include company name, city, state and dates of employment, in addition to your job title. You may also want to include some details about the organizations where you have worked. If you have had more than one position with a company, lead with the last position you had while there. When listing your employment history, add achievements and experience in a bulleted format. Your first bullet for each position should always be your best bullet.  Be sure to focus on results and accomplishments when stating what you did in each position.  Remember, your resume is a marketing tool, not an autobiography.  Also, keep in mind, there is no need to go back any further than 10 years when listing employment history on your resume.  Although we would hope that age discrimination would not be a factor, going back too far would indicate the length of one's career and estimated age.  One way to add relevant experience is to insert it as additional relevant experience with no dates.

When listing your education, lead with the most recent information first.  For example, if you have recently received an industry or job related certification, list that first and then list your college education.  This is where adding dates can be a little tricky.  If your education is recent, it is likely you will want to add dates.  If you graduated from college more than 10-15 years ago, forego adding the dates to avoid age discrimination. In either case, be consistent.

Prospective employers like to see professional affiliations and/or community involvement.  Therefore, by all means, list any professional organizations that you are associated with and any volunteer or community involvement as well.

Be sure to proofread everything on your resume.  It is advisable to have someone with proofreading skills take a look also, to ensure there are no misspellings, typos, grammar and spacing errors.

DON'T GIVE UP. GREAT THINGS TAKE TIME.

# Step 3 - Action Plan

**Is my resume strategic and professional?**

**Do I need to reconfigure my resume?**

**Do I have my Employment History listed appropriately?**

**Do I have my Certifications and Education listed appropriately?**

**Have I included my Professional Affiliations and Community Involvement?**

**Have I proofread my resume and had someone with proofreading skills review it also?**

**For professional assistance with your resume, contact one of our Career Strategists at www.mclainenterprisesllc.com.**

10 Steps to Landing Your Dream Job

# Step 4 - Update Professional/Business Network Profiles (e.g., LinkedIn, Opportunity, SHRM, ASA)

Although you may have several Professional Network Profiles, we are going to focus on LinkedIn. Your LinkedIn profile is a very important marketing tool, just like your resume. It must mirror your resume. Prospective employers will view your LinkedIn profile, especially if they are interested in pursuing you further.

It is good to have connections relative to your industry and interests. Your interests should correlate with your career and industry. Don't be afraid to ask for recommendations from colleagues and feel free to give recommendations as well. Be sure to list your accomplishments and any volunteer experience. Posts articles and posts, like and comment, as well as share others' posts and articles.

If we're growing, we're always going to be out of our comfort zone.

John C. Maxwell

## Step 4 - Action Plan

**Is my LinkedIn profile set up in a professional manner?**

**Does my LinkedIn profile match the information on my resume?**

**Have I personalized my LinkedIn profile URL?**

**Have I added my professional email address in the contact area?**

**Have I reached out to connect with others in my career field/industry?**

**Have I listed my accomplishments, interests and volunteer experience?**

**Have I recommended my peers and colleagues?**

**Have I asked for recommendations from my peers and colleagues?**

**For professional assistance with your LinkedIn profile, contact one of our Career Strategists at www.mclainenterprisesllc.com.**

10 Steps to Landing Your Dream Job

# Step 5 – Do A Targeted Job Search

Target the companies you are most interested in working for and the positions relative to your experience and/or education. Determine whether you want to work in a corporate environment or the non-profit sector. Do you prefer large companies, middle size or smaller start ups and/or entrepreneurial companies? Do your research on the structure of the companies you identify. Check the reviews of past and present employees. Find out as much as you can about their financial stability, length of time in existence, mergers and acquisitions. Attentively read through the various pages of their websites and any related news articles.

After doing your research, once you have identified your short list of companies you are interested in, be mindful of the various locations and the commuting distance to ensure each site will be feasible for you.

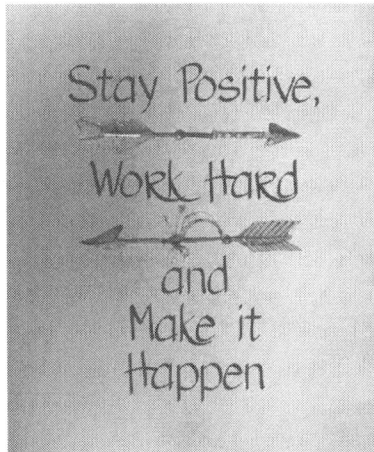

Stay Positive, Work Hard and Make it Happen

## Step 5 – Action Plan

**Have I determined what type of company I would like to work for (corporate, industrial, non-profit)?**

**Do I prefer to work at a large or small company? Why?**

**Have I done my research on the structure and culture of my short list of companies?**

**What is the company structure and culture like?**

**Where are the various locations?**

**Is the location I am interested in a feasible commute for me?**

# Step 6 – Applying for Your Dream Job

Typically, you may not know who the position of Your Dream Job reports to, but if you do, that can be a great advantage. If you have this information, send your resume, along with a cover letter, directly to the hiring manager. Reference any related information in your letter, such as who referred you, how you found about the position, etc. Be sure to sell yourself in your cover letter so the manager will look forward to finding out more about you and your related experience when he/she reads your resume. Don't make your letter too long, but be sure to include enough information to pique interest. Close your letter by thanking the hiring manager for their time and consideration.

If you are not aware of the hiring manager for Your Dream Job, submit your resume and cover letter, or submit your application online to Human Resources through the normal application process. Keep in mind, search engines identify key words listed in the job description, so be sure to have those words in your resume/application. For example, you may be a Recruiter, but if the position title is Talent Acquisition Specialist, which essentially is the same thing, don't change your title, but change your description to reflect that you are responsible for talent acquisition.

focus on the goal...

@JUSTSAYINGIRL

# Step 6 – Action Plan

**Do I know the name of the hiring manager? If yes, can I use this to my advantage and apply directly to him/her?**

**Have I thoroughly read the job description?**

**Do I qualify for this position?**

**Is this position a good match to my experience and education?**

**Does the described environment and company culture seem like a good fit for me?**

**Have I prepared an appropriate cover letter?**

**Do I need to interchange any key words to ensure a relevant experience match when applying for this position?**

**For professional assistance with your cover letter or application process, contact one of our Career Strategists at www.mclainenterprisesllc.com.**

# 10 Steps to Landing Your Dream Job

## Step 7 – Preparing for the Interview

Once you have been invited to interview for your Dream Job, you want to be sure to properly and adequately prepare. Do your research of the company and the person/people with whom you will be interviewing. You want to exhibit your knowledge of the company, in addition to your expertise, and how it relates to the position and company to which you have applied. Know some key facts that you have obtained from your research that you can share when appropriate, e.g., sales for the last quarter, acquirement of XYZ company last month. You can also use this information as you prepare your questions that you will be asking.

This is the time that you ensure you have your professional portfolio (and a good writing pen), with notes from your research. Also be sure to list any questions that you may want to ask during your interview.

EVEN THE
SMALLEST
STEPS
MOVE YOU
FORWARD.

OPRAH WINFREY

## Step 7 – Action Plan

**Have I done my research of the company and the people I will be meeting with?**

**Am I able to exhibit my knowledge of the company if I am asked what do I know about ABC Company?**

**Do I have my professional portfolio and good writing pen ready to go?**

# Step 8 – The Interview

Having prepared your professional outfit the night before, will eliminate unnecessary stress the morning of the interview. Be sure to have your professional portfolio in hand with questions you have previously prepared to ask, along with your notes from your research to help with recollection. Greet everyone you meet with a firm handshake, ensuring you make direct eye contact. Be sure to sit up straight to ensure the right body language. Be attentive and answer questions directly and appropriately. Do not ramble. If you are unsure of a question that is asked, do not try to wing it. Ask for them to repeat the question or for more clarity so you can answer the question with understanding.

Your first interview may be by phone or video. If this is the case, be sure to schedule it for a time when you can be in a quiet atmosphere with no distractions. Some employers will determine to move forward with candidates after a successful professional conversation.

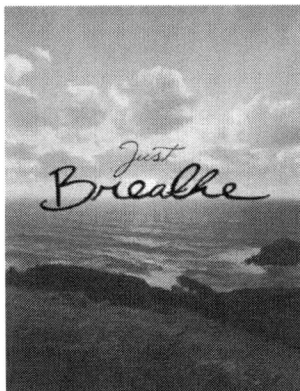

# Step 8 – Action Plan

**Have you prepared your professional outfit the night before your interview?**

**Do you have your questions ready that you would like to ask?**

**Do you know the appropriate questions to ask?**

**Have you prepared for your interview with a friend by doing a mock interview?**

**Have you checked directions and how long it will take you to get to your interview?**

**Have you done a trial run to the location so you know about parking and what landmarks to look for?**

**If your first interview is by phone or video, have you prepared your quiet atmosphere with no distractions and a background free of clutter?**

**For professional assistance with Interview Preparation, contact one of our Career Strategists at www.mclainenterprisesllc.com.**

# 10 Steps to Landing Your Dream Job

## Step 9 – After the Interview

Preferably within a few hours after the interview, or by the end of the day send "thank you" emails to everyone you met with. This gesture goes a long way with interviewers and decision makers. Be sure to get a business card from everyone you met with to make this a seamless process.

You want to ensure to the decision makers that you value their time. Thanking them for taking the time to meet with you regarding ABC position is a great way to display your appreciation.

Your personality will show through your writing style. Do not add inspirational or funny quotes. Be sure to keep your signature clean and professional.

**MAKE IT SIMPLE,
BUT SIGNIFICANT.**

DON DRAPER

## Step 9 - Action Plan

**Did you remember to get a business card from everyone you met with at your interview?**

**Did you send your "thank you" emails to all decision makers no later than the close of the business day?**

## Step 10 – Landing Your Dream Job

After acing the interview and following up with your "thank you" emails, connect with your prospective employer on LinkedIn to stay engaged. If they told you during the interview when they intend to make a decision, wait for that time frame before following up. Ultimately you won't have to, if you are the selected candidate!

## Step 10 – Action Plan

**Did you connect with your prospective employer on LinkedIn?**

# Conclusion

When you are offered Your Dream Job, do not accept a salary you are not pleased with. There will not be a second chance for this part of the process.

Some companies a) disclose the salary range right up front, before you interview and that is great. It allows you to make an informed decision to determine if you will pursue the opportunity and no one's time is wasted. Other companies b) have a salary range in mind that they share at the interview with viable candidates. And then there are c) those who will not disclose the salary range, but want you to tell them what salary you are seeking.

When given a salary range, if it is within the salary range that you are seeking, this can be a win-win situation. So when they ask you what salary you are looking for, you simply answer that your salary requirement is within their range.

When you are not given a salary, but are asked what salary you are seeking, a great response is to ask "What is the salary range for the position?" If they tell you, you can then let them know that your desired salary is within that range. If they play hardball, and will not indicate any range, you can give them a range, not an exact amount.

After discussing the compensation package, which may include, health benefits, time off, pension plan, commissions, bonuses, etc., if the bottom line of your offered salary meets with your satisfaction great. If the extended salary does not meet with your satisfaction, ask if it is negotiable. If it is negotiable, negotiate another range, not a specific amount. It is good if you can come to an agreeable amount.

Once you have negotiated your salary and perks, it is alright to ask for a day or two to think about it, if you do not want to give your decision right away. Keep in mind this will be your salary for at least one year, unless they have put other parameters in place. Be sure to get back to your potential employer of Your Dream Job, in the timeframe that you said you would.

If you decide to accept the offer, be sure to get an official offer in writing from your potentially new employer, before giving notice to your current employer.

CONGRATULATIONS! You are well on your way to Landing Your Dream Job!

Wishing You Success

# Employment Contacts

**Company Name/Location:**
**Contact Person:**
**Position Title:**
**Salary:**
**Perks:**
**Additional Information:**


**Company Name/Location:**
**Contact Person:**
**Position Title:**
**Salary:**
**Perks:**
**Additional Information:**


**Company Name/Location:**
**Contact Person:**
**Position Title:**
**Salary:**
**Perks:**
**Additional Information:**

**Company Name/Location:**
**Contact Person:**
**Position Title:**
**Salary:**
**Perks:**
**Additional Information:**


**Company Name/Location:**
**Contact Person:**
**Position Title:**
**Salary:**
**Perks:**
**Additional Information:**


**Company Name/Location:**
**Contact Person:**
**Position Title:**
**Salary:**
**Perks:**
**Additional Information:**

**Company Name/Location:**
**Contact Person:**
**Position Title:**
**Salary:**
**Perks:**
**Additional Information:**


**Company Name/Location:**
**Contact Person:**
**Position Title:**
**Salary:**
**Perks:**
**Additional Information:**


**Company Name/Location:**
**Contact Person:**
**Position Title:**
**Salary:**
**Perks:**
**Additional Information:**

**Company Name/Location:**
**Contact Person:**
**Position Title:**
**Salary:**
**Perks:**
**Additional Information:**


**Company Name/Location:**
**Contact Person:**
**Position Title:**
**Salary:**
**Perks:**
**Additional Information:**


**Company Name/Location:**
**Contact Person:**
**Position Title:**
**Salary:**
**Perks:**
**Additional Information:**

# Additional Notes

_____

_____

_____

_____

_____

_____

_____

_____

_____

_____

_____

_____

_____

_____

_____

_____

# 10 Steps to Landing Your Dream Job

_____

_____

_____

_____

_____

_____

_____

_____

_____

_____

_____

_____

_____

_____

_____

_____

_____

_____

# About the Author

C. Renee McLain loves to Encourage, Enlighten and Empower others, thereby equipping them in the various aspects and stages of their lives. She is a Certified Life Coach, Career Strategist, Mentor, and Motivator. As the business owner of McLain Enterprises, LLC and corporate executive, her combined diverse experience of 20+ years in the Human Resources industry has afforded her a career of Coaching, Mentoring and Motivating others. Cooperatively, with her gift of Organizational Excellence, she equips primarily women, with the proper tools to develop and excel in reaching their fullest potential.

Renee is actively involved with several professional and charitable organizations including American Business Women's Association (ABWA), American Staffing Association (ASA), National Association of Women

Owned Small Businesses (NAWOSB), Destiny's Daughters of Promise, and Victorious Ladies of Virtue.

Renee is happily married to Robert J. McLain, Sr. They are blessed with one son, Robert, Jr. and two grandchildren, Robert, III and Gabriella.

For more information about Renee or if you would like to contact her for a coaching session or speaking engagement, she can be reached at:

P.O. Box 2157 ♦ Villa Rica, GA 30180
770-459-0615
www.mclainenterprisesllc.com
mclainenterprises.ga@gmail.com
www.facebook.com/McLainEnterprisesLLC

10 Steps to Landing Your Dream Job

10 Steps to Landing Your Dream Job

10 Steps to Landing Your Dream Job

Made in the USA
Columbia, SC
30 May 2017